SUMMARY OF

Educated

-A Memoir-

by Tara Westover

ISBN: 9781719858496.

TABLE OF CONTENTS

Introduction

Tara Westover was born to Mormon survivalists in Idaho and was only familiar with the rough life of the mountains. She and some of her siblings did not go to school. They did not even have records. Their father prepared for a day when the government would come to persecute them. Tara and her siblings were raised to fear the government, doctors, and anything that went against the views of her father.

Part One

Chapter 1: Choose the Good

Tara's paternal family had been living at the base of Buck Peak for five decades. Her paternal grandmother lived nearby and her maternal grandmother resided 15 miles south. Her father clashed with his mother quite frequently. He also habitually recited the Bible to them. They were not allowed to have some basic things like milk since their father believed that milk was connected to Satan. This made Tara go to her grandmother's place to have her share of milk.

Since Tara's paternal grandfather was quite frail and could not bear Idaho's winters, her grandparents spent winter elsewhere. Tara wanted to run away with them.

Chapter 2: The Midwife

On her father's suggestion to exercise more self-dependence, her mother started helping the local midwife. Her first case was extremely complicated since the umbilical cord circled the baby's neck. The outcome was normal but it disturbed her. Like Tara's dad, some others in the vicinity did not find going to hospitals acceptable either. Mother helped the midwife, Judy, with some other cases too. When Judy left the area, Mother had to assume the role of a midwife despite not actually wanting to. She started developing a fondness for midwifery later.

Midwifery transformed their lives since Mother could take them out for meals because of it. She even purchased a phone and tools to support her work. Further, when Luke wanted to have a birth certificate at 15, she decided to get all of her children's birth certificates made. It was a challenge to get Tara's birth certificate made since there was a conflict regarding her birth date. At the age of 9, she received a Delayed Certificate of Birth. Further, she accompanied her mother on a case but did not care for the experience.

Chapter 3: Cream Shoes

Tara's parents went by the names Gene and Faye. Even though Faye's mother was prim and proper, Faye was different. She liked the fact that Gene was a combination of mischief and seriousness.

Gene's father was short-tempered. His mother was a working lady but Gene believed that a woman belongs at home. He was in charge of the farm during his childhood. When Gene and Faye met, Gene was quite a jolly fellow. He seemed to be more sober than others his age and there was a distinct quality about him. Faye's brother Lynn disapproved of Gene. In fact, Faye's family as a whole was not too happy with the engagement. While growing up, Tara did not get to know a lot about her mother's family. Her father rarely went to their maternal grandparents' place. However, Faye's younger sister, Aunt Angie, was different. She still wished to meet Faye. Faye's mother passed away three years ago.

Tara's father changed considerably from the jolly guy he used to be when he married her mother. He turned into someone full of paranoia, always gathering goods and ammunition to be prepared for the time when the government would come after them. Tara's siblings include Tony, Shawn, Tyler, Luke, Audrey and Richard. Tara is the youngest. A majority of them had a home birth with help from midwives.

Tara's father was not always as paranoid. He kept getting worse and eventually made her brothers bid goodbye to school. The next step for him was to cease to register and renew various things. He started collecting food next. Tara figured out later in life that his mental illness was never diagnosed, let alone treated.

Chapter 4: Apache Women

When their grandparents were spending winter in Arizona and Tara's family was on its way to their mobile home, their station wagon met with an accident when Tyler was driving and he fell asleep. Dad lost his temper on knowing that his mother was consulting a doctor. He went on to blame her for being an Illuminati agent. He started behaving in such a way that Tara's mother could not bear to be in the same room as him. On their journey back home, they had another accident. Mother had a brain injury as a result of this accident so severe that she could not even identify her children sometimes. They still did not consult a doctor. Tyler held himself accountable for the accident and everything that happened in its wake. Tara did not consider anyone to be accountable for it and approached it in the form of the bigger picture.

Chapter 5: Honest Dirt

After a month, Tyler declared that he was saying goodbye to attend college. Tony and Shawn had already bid adieu by that time. Tyler had experienced speech issues and was unique among the siblings. He had a preference for books and calmness. While his brothers were busy wrestling, he let music give him peace. Tara had begun listening to music with him as well. Tyler had enrolled himself in school in 8th grade and this made him yearn for learning in spite of several hurdles and challenges. Dad chose to remain in denial for a period of time after Tyler's college declaration but Tyler went ahead to leave for unfamiliar territory.

When they were children, Dad had been more interested in teaching them pragmatic skills while Mother tried to homeschool them. The most difficult to teach was Luke because of his learning disability. Mother let go of her passion eventually and the children started learning what they wished to or were interested in.

Tara had very little discipline and by the age of 10, she had just learned Morse code on Dad's insistence. Tara was devoid of manners to the point that she did not even wash her hands after using the toilet even though her maternal grandmother objected to the terrible habit.

Chapter 6: Shield and Buckler

After turning 15, Audrey got a driver's license, started doing jobs here and there and became independent. Their family dynamics started transforming. Since Tara's three eldest brothers had left by then, Dad could not develop hay sheds any longer and restricted himself to scraping. Luke became his biggest support. Richard and Tara assumed their role as side helpers. The junkyard was brutal and like others, Tara also experienced injuries since her father threw stuff around. Mother got better, having a fewer number of headaches and not restricting herself to the basement as frequently. She started serving as a midwife again but needed being managed. She found her calling in blending oils for healing, examining muscles, and beginning energy work. She learned spirituality in healing.

Tara became fascinated by studying because of Tyler. Richard also studied encyclopedias in his spare time. Tara studied the Book of Mormon and other scriptures. After facing a bad work injury, she told Dad that she wished to attend school. Dad reacted by informing her that they follow the Lord's commandments. He let her know that she was not being his daughter by saying things like that.

Chapter 7: The Lord Will Provide

It did not rain the subsequent summer. Luke and Richard assisted Dad. Once, when Tara was 10 and Mother was not home, Luke's gasoline-soaked trousers caught fire at work. They differed in their accounts of what followed. Tara provided treatment to Luke and Dad went to the site to contain the fire. Luke experienced intense pain and lost a considerable amount of skin and flesh from his leg. Tara wished to give him morphine even though she did not care for hospital drugs because of Dad's lessons. After coming back, Mother provided further treatment to Luke.

Chapter 8: Tiny Harlots

Tara, 11 then, realized that if she wished to follow Audrey's footsteps to stay away from home she would need to find a job. When she asked the gas station owner, Myrna, for permission to place a notice, Myrna informed her that her daughter needed a babysitter. Tara started babysitting for Myrna's daughter Mary. Her next job was to pack cashews for a man. Mary made her join her sister Caroline's dance class. While other girls wore pretty clothes, Tara wore boyish ones. Caroline convinced Mother to buy Tara a dress that Tara found to be devoid of modesty. Tara was supposed to conceal it from Dad.

When Mother did not like the design of the Christmas costume, Caroline made sweatshirts for Tara's class. Dad came to the recital as well and Tara could not even perform correctly because of her fear of him. Dad yelled while returning home and considered the class to be Satan's work. He even persuaded Mother. She later made it possible for Tara to be part of a choir. When Tara sang in the choir and people adored it, Dad felt proud. He even permitted her to audition for the play *Annie* in town.

Chapter 9: Perfect in His Generations

Tara sang in the play in 1999. Dad's paranoia worsened. He was obsessed with Y2K and thought everything would end because of the government's mistake. He warned others and told them to stockpile food as well. Their family collected food in a root cellar.

Tara's rehearsals at the Worm Creek Opera House provided her with her first chance to meet those who attended schools and consulted doctors. Dad let Tara audition for other plays. On Dad's suggestion, she stood with her mouth open under the sun for a month to treat her tonsils but it did not improve matters.

One of the people she met at Worm Creek was Charles, who considered her singing to be top class. With the year coming to a close, Dad's paranoia concerning Y2K reached an all-time high. Dad stayed glued to the TV for long hours on the night of December 31st and when nothing happened, he was disappointed.

Chapter 10: Shield of Feathers

Since 2000 turned out to be a regular year, it saddened Dad since he did not have anything to anticipate. Mother announced another Arizona trip. Tara went with Richard, Audrey, and her parents since Luke was busy. Arizona's sunny climate made Dad cheerful like earlier. Grandmother was tired of the treatment for bone marrow cancer.

On their way back home, they met with an accident and an ambulance and the police arrived. Dad made a call to Rob and Diane Hardy after failing to contact his sons. After the accident, Tara could not turn her neck one day. Her condition got worse and she was unable to stand without support. The energy specialist called by her mother did not help. She stayed in bed for a month, being was still unable to move her neck. Shawn made a visit and informed her that what she needed was a chiropractor. He assisted her to move her neck and she began seeing him as some form of a shield.

Chapter 11: Instinct

Tara and Shawn tamed horses since their paternal grandfather auctioned horses every year. Shawn began spending more time at home. He dropped Tara off to her lessons. Once, when they were both riding horses, Tara came too close to the newly saddled mare Shawn was riding and the two horses became hysterical. The situation got difficult but both the siblings successfully controlled their horses somehow.

Chapter 12: Fish Eyes

Tony's wife got ill and he asked Shawn to take care of his rig for some time since she needed bed rest. Tara went with Shawn. They went trucking to places including Las Vegas, Washington State, etc. The trip was quite enjoyable.

A girl named Sadie from the Opera House began frequenting the junkyard for Shawn. Shawn developed feelings for her too. He told Tara that Sadie has fish eyes. He got jealous on seeing Sadie with Charles and punished her by not talking to her. She asked the boys at school to stop talking to her because of this. Shawn further punished her by asking her to fetch things for him reiteratively. This seemed unfair to Tara and when she retaliated by spilling water over Shawn, he punished her cruelly in the washroom.

Chapter 13: Silence in the Churches

Three days after the fall of the twin towers, Audrey, 19, married Benjamin. Dad announced that his sons would go to war. Tara dreaded the war and forgave Shawn at the wedding for the bathroom episode.

Tara's body was transforming and she did not wish to stay a child. Dad criticized women for dressing and acting in a certain manner, which dictated Tara's thinking for a long time with her believing that she was becoming the wrong type of woman.

Shawn had bad things to say when Tara began wearing makeup. Charles told Tara he loved Sadie and Shawn criticized Tara for talking to Charles. Shawn and Sadie went through a breakup and Shawn started seeing an old girlfriend. It angered Shawn when Sadie said yes to Charles's date. Shawn treated Tara brutally since he considered her to be a slut but Tyler arrived and saved her. But Tara's thinking had been affected by Dad's expectations of how a woman should behave to such an extent that she asked Shawn not to let her be a woman like others. He pledged his assistance. Tyler asked her to attend school since BYU takes homeschoolers.

Chapter 14: My Feet No Longer Touch Earth

Shawn and the others became occupied once Dad had a contract. Tara's boss Randy showed her how to use the internet. Tyler asked Tara to purchase books and get ready for the ACT exam. Tyler convinced Tara to apply for college since it would allow her to study music. She visited BYU's website and purchased an ACT study guide. When Mother could not assist her with algebra anymore, she went on to purchase a big algebra textbook. She asked Dad to assist her with trigonometry. Tyler taught her later.

When Shawn fell at work, he had a severe internal brain injury. Tara bade adieu to work and took up the role of his attendant. Sadie became a visitor. Doctors informed Mother that Shawn's personality had changed because of the accident and he might stay aggressive and volatile. Tara told herself that he had never been violent before the accident and the accident made him that way.

Chapter 15: No More a Child

Dad told Tara about God's impending wrath because of her decision to attend college. Mother told her she always expected her to go. Since Shawn could not help Dad anymore, the construction business went downhill. With Dad returning to scraping, Tara joined him since she required the money. She was afraid of the ACT test since a huge number of people pursued BYU. After the exam, Tara was sure that she had failed. She found her aspirations ridiculous. Her test results arrived and even though she had not received the required score of 27 for BYU, she had received a 22, which showed possibilities for Tara.

Shawn returned to work and Tara and Shawn worked for a month on the Shear, a deadly machine purchased by Dad.

Chapter 16: Disloyal Man, Disobedient Heaven

Tara drove the crane on Shawn's determination with construction beginning on the milking barn in Oneida. Dad did not like it but Shawn stood up to him like always. While Tara was studying to prepare for retaking the ACT, Shawn guaranteed that she was smart enough to get 27. Shawn's had an accident on his motorbike. The hole in Shawn's head enabled Tara to see his brain at the site. Dad wanted her to bring Shawn home but she took him to the hospital. The doctor thought the damage was not too bad and stitched the wound.

Tara got a score of 28 on the ACT the second time and got into BYU. When Tara and Mother came back from their apartment hunt, Dad threw a huge tantrum. Tyler was also getting married then.

Part Two

Chapter 17: To Keep It Holy

Mother took Tara to her apartment in the city on New Year's Day. Tara did not like the immodest dressing of her first housemate Shannon. She faced further disappointment because of the ways of all her housemates. Classes began and Tara set foot in a classroom for the first time ever at the age of 17. Tara did not know what the Holocaust was and when her professor asked her not to joke about it, she read up about the Holocaust and was embarrassed of her ignorance.

When her housemates wished to see a movie after church, Tara refused since she did not believe in watching movies on Sunday. She even thought she had contradicted the Lord by joining Sunday school. Tara's overall courses included religion, American history, music, and English.

Chapter 18: Blood and Feathers

The dynamics between Tara and her housemates were strained since Tara did not take part in cleaning up the house, despite things getting rotten in the refrigerator. Tara did not even wash her hands after going to the toilet and this astonished everyone in the house.

When Tara did not pass her western civilization exam, she did not wish to share this with her family. When she shared it with her father over the phone, he comforted her and assured her that he would assist with the money. She was moved when he asked her to visit home. For her next western civilization exam, she studied with her classmate Vanessa. When Vanessa advised her to read the textbook rather than just pay attention to the pictures, Tara was surprised. Following the advice helped her pass the exam with a B. She began receiving A's by the time the semester ended. Her professor did not include the grades from the first exam so her initial failure did not count in the end.

Chapter 19: In the Beginning

Tara returned to Buck's Peak when the semester finished. She required money and resumed her job at Stokes. Dad asked her to work for him that summer but she refused because she did not want to go back to where she initiated her journey. Dad still wanted her to work for him. When she called Tyler for help, he wanted to help her but she misunderstood him and hanged up. She left Stokes and started working for Dad. Shawn seemed quite transformed and calm. He was preparing for the GED and shared his aspirations of studying law.

They went to the Opera House and met Charles. Charles asked her out but the movie they watched together was vulgar. He called her after it and they bonded. Tara purchased some girly clothes and when she went out with Charles in those clothes, it felt different. They started going out often. When Charles touched her hand for the first time ever, she brushed it away since she still remembered her father's words regarding how a woman should behave.

Tara got A's in all subjects barring western civilization and this bore the promise of a 50% scholarship.

Chapter 20: Recitals of the Fathers

Dad believed Tara was turning into someone pretentious and increased the complexity of her work so that she would recall her origins. Shawn saw eye to eye with him on this. She also comprehended now how wrong it was of Shawn to call her 'nigger' when she blackened her face at work and was more aware of her family's ignorance.

Chapter 21: Skullcap

Dad was unable to pay Tara's BYU semester fees. Charles gave her medication for an earache. It made her anxious to take the pill but she did take it, this being the first time ever that she had medicine in her life. She took Dad's new car to college since he had failed to assist her completely in paying her fees. She then moved into an apartment with Jenni, Megan, and Robin. Algebra gave her a lot of anxiety until she discussed it with her professor. She made plans to study algebra over Thanksgiving. She developed stomach ulcers but did not consult a doctor.

Chapter 22: What We Whispered and What We Screamed

Tara went back home for Thanksgiving. Shawn kept bullying her and even became physically violent with her in front of Charles. This affected her relationship with Charles as well. She finally started acknowledging Shawn negatively in her journals. When she went back to college, she managed to get an A through hard work and determination.

Chapter 23: I'm from Idaho

Tara realized she would not have money for the subsequent semester. She experienced a severe toothache as well. She started seeing a bishop for counseling sessions. The bishop made her apply for a governmental grant, which improved matters considerably. It was a big step for Tara since her family had strictly been against such grants. She got her course books and the tooth treatment.

Chapter 24: A Knight, Errant

Having money to support herself was new and it enabled her to focus on other things. She became extremely interested in her studies. A psychology lecture made her come to the realization that Dad likely suffered from bipolar disorder. She selected the topic as her project since it really captivated her interest. She moved into a new apartment and met Nick at a new church, who really caught her fancy. Nick convinced her to consult a doctor when she began suffering from a throat infection.

Chapter 25: The Work of Sulphur

She went back home when Audrey called to inform her that Dad had been in an accident. Dad had experienced severe burns but refused medical treatment. Mother helped him with her herbs. The severe burns made Tara think that Dad might pass away at any moment. However, he survived.

Chapter 26: Waiting for Moving Water

When Shawn announced his engagement with Emily, Tara became scared for the girl. This made her accompany Shawn and Emily on a long horse ride and camping trip. Dad had a chance to learn about her life. She returned to college and the gap between her and Nick started widening. She could not share things with Nick despite wanting to. After Shawn and Emily's wedding, she broke up with Nick because she did not feel open enough to share the truth about her family with him.

Chapter 27: If I Were a Woman

Tara no longer felt interested in music and started studying politics, history, and world affairs. Her professor guided her regarding a University of Cambridge program and she applied there. Emily got pregnant and Mother treated her when she experienced problems in her pregnancy. When Tara got into Cambridge, she faced several issues in getting a passport but finally got it. Emily gave birth to Peter prematurely. Gene finally recovered from his accident.

Chapter 28: Pygmalion

At King's College, Cambridge, Tara's supervisor was Professor Steinberg, a well-known Holocaust historian. He was quite impressed by her. When he saw her work, he remarked that she had the ability to continue studying further. Tara still found the institution daunting and did not feel like she belonged.

Chapter 29: Graduation

She applied for the Gates Cambridge Scholarship on Professor Steinberg's encouragement but never believed that she would get it. She received a yes and was able to clear her interview. When her parents surprised her by visiting her, she took them out. She realized that in her new environment, her father's hold over her mind had weakened. Her parents were not larger than life to her any longer. They were quite late getting to her graduation ceremony because of a conflict with Dad.

Part Three

Chapter 30: Hand of the Almighty

The next chapter in Tara's life was Trinity College, Cambridge. She came to realize that the other students at the college surpassed her in knowledge by miles. She did not comprehend a huge number of things. For example, she felt ignorant on the topic of feminism and dedicated herself to study the subject. She realized that there are no specific requirements from a woman and she could be anything she wanted *and* be a woman. She returned to Idaho on Christmas. Richard and his new family showed a new side of her kin. Her mother's herbal business flourished.

Chapter 31: Tragedy Then Farce

Tara started getting accustomed to Cambridge after being intimidated initially. She worked hard at college and visited Rome with friends after her finals. Audrey shared in an email how Shawn had been violent toward her. Audrey wanted to ask their parents to save Emily from him. Tara agreed but told her to wait.

Chapter 32: A Brawling Woman in a Wide House

Tara returned to Idaho where her grandmother passed away after some time. Dad became extremely disturbed. After the funeral, Mother stood up to Dad when he told her to manage her "wifely" duties.

Chapter 33: Sorcery of Physics

Audrey attempted to gain Tara's support against Shawn's abuse and this made Tara feel guilty for not being there for her sister when she returned to Cambridge. Drew also attended Cambridge for his Master's Degree and Tara got busier. Tara tried harder because she saw the likelihood of getting into the PhD program. She chose the topic of Mormonism from a social viewpoint. When she went back to Idaho for Christmas, their parents had reached a truce. She met Shawn and Luke. Shawn had bad things to say about Audrey for the supposed "lies" she was telling about him. He did not hurt Tara since she did not acknowledge her participation in the topic.

Chapter 34: The Substance of Things

When Tara complained to Dad about Shawn's threats against Audrey, he refused to believe her and asked for proof. She could not believe it. Dad asked Shawn to defend himself against her allegations and this made Tara extremely frustrated. Tara had to lie to save herself but Shawn still threatened her by passing her a knife with blood on it. She left for Salt Lake City the next day. On her way there, she saw the blood of a dog named Diego outside Shawn's trailer. She realized that Shawn had taken his anger out on the helpless animal.

Chapter 35: West of the Sun

Tara stayed with Drew in Salt Lake City for the remainder of the holidays. After returning to Cambridge, she knew that Shawn would soon realize the lie she had told. Soon enough, he started communicating his anger in emails and phone calls to her. He even threatened to kill her. She phoned her parents to let them know about his violent threats but they refused to believe her. She could not believe it when Audrey admitted that she had told Dad that it was Tara who was at fault.

Chapter 36: Four Long Arms, Whirling

Tara went to Harvard in September and became increasingly engrossed in her studies. She did not expect anything of her family anymore. It seemed to her that they were not going to accept her for who she was and she let go of them. Her parents surprised her by visiting her. They had come to her to make her realize her mistakes and give her the chance to try to redeem herself. Dad wanted to give her his blessing to make the devil leave her but Tara refused since she had come to a point where she considered her own mind to be more significant. This did not make her parents too happy.

Chapter 37: Gambling for Redemption

Tara was so disturbed in the subsequent days that she experienced anxiety. She lost interest in her studies completely and her future at the institution was at risk. She came back home to gain some peace by seeking her parents' blessing. Back home, when she needed to email Drew, she read the correspondence between Erin and Mother. She realized that Mother was no different from Dad and believed that Tara was doing the devil's work. Tara left. Tyler called her later and sided with her.

Chapter 38: Family

Tara believed that Tyler would treat her the same way as Audrey and go against her. However, Tyler stood firm to support her against their parents. Tara felt grateful for his support. When she finally saw a counselor, it brought a considerable amount of comfort and peace to her. She took charge of her matters once more and her academic journey blossomed. Her thesis topic included family among other things. After finishing her doctorate, she moved to London with Drew.

Chapter 39: Watching the Buffalo

Tara did not deny the problems her family had but still returned to see those members of the family who would accept her for who she was. She met Tyler and her maternal family. Tara, Tyler, and Richard stayed away from their parents' beliefs and views while the remainder of the siblings still suffered under their hold. Her family's herbal business was still growing.

Chapter 40: Educated

Tara has not seen her parents or the other siblings that are again under their influence. She is in touch with Tyler, Tony, and Richard. She was able to transform herself because of what she chose for herself, which educated her. She does not mind the gap between her father and herself since it is in her best interest to keep it that way. In retrospect, she believes that what assisted her in healing and moving forward was her reiterative acknowledgement to herself about the problems engulfing her home. She might return to Buck's Peak someday but does not know when.

Conclusion

Tara Westover's tale is a story of survival and struggle. She had a challenging upbringing in an environment full of paranoia. However, she was able to rise from the hurdles and polish herself into a highly educated individual with the assistance of her will power and determination. Her story pays homage to the fact that when a person decides to do something and put his or her mind to it, he or she can truly achieve anything.

Check out other books

We thank you for buying the book and really hope that it will benefit you. We also want to provide you with the best summary books possible.

1- Summary of *How to Win Friends and Influence People* by **Dale Carnegie**

Reference link: https://www.amazon.com/dp/B07G1K8MWW

2- Summary of *The Subtle Art of Not Giving a F*ck* by **Mark Manson:** A counterintuitive approach to living a good life

Reference link: https://www.amazon.com/dp/B07GC5SXXM

3- Summary of *The 7 Habits of Highly Effective People* by **Stephen R. Covey:** Powerful Lessons in Personal Change

Reference link: https://www.amazon.com/dp/B07FM3B1B6

4- Summary of *The Diabetes Code* by **Dr. Jason Fung** : Prevent and Reverse Type 2 Diabetes Naturally

Reference link: https://www.amazon.com/dp/B07HDTRCFK

5- Summary of *The Obesity Code* by **Jason Fung**

This book will actually help you lose weight by making you understand the benefits of intermittent fasting. This is a practical guide with evidence to support the main ideas.

Reference link: https://www.amazon.com/dp/B07H39XJ6M

6-SUMMARY: *Measure What Matters* by **John Doerr**

In *Measure What Matters*, John Doerr defines and makes a case for OKRs (objectives and key results) to direct a company toward success.

*Reference link: https://www.amazon.com/dp/B07G9KJWDS

7- Summary of *Unlimited Memory* by **Kevin Horsley**: How to Use Advanced Learning Strategies to Learn Faster, Remember More and be More Productive

Reference link: https://www.amazon.com/dp/B07FNXM36T

***To find out more about other summary books, please visit the Amazon Author Page . We will be adding more titles soon so please click the "+Follow" button to stay up-to-date.

THANKS FOR READING!

Made in the USA
San Bernardino, CA
30 September 2018